A Photographic Journey around the USA
During the years: 1997 – 1998.

By: Carl R. Hussey, B.A. PGCert.

A Photographic Journey around the USA.
During the years: 1997 – 1998.

I invite you to join me on a very special photographic journey around the USA (The United States of America), during my travels between my Keele University undergraduate degree semesters during 1997 and 1998. It really was the trip of a lifetime, and I hope that my pictures and brief narratives help to inspire you to discover America for yourself! It is a fabulous country with a unique and special history, great towns and cities and wonderful National Parks. So let's discover my own special journey around this very special country: The Good Old USA!

By: Carl R. Hussey, B.A. PGCert.

(c) Carl R. Hussey, 2021.

A Photographic Journey around the USA.
During the years: 1997 – 1998.

Dedication & Acknowledgements.

This book is dedicated to the many, many people that I have met during my travels around the USA and the wider world over the past few years, and of course to my Family and Friends. Travelling certainly does open you up to all kinds of interesting and exciting possibilities and experiences, and you are left with memories that will last a lifetime.

The USA during 1997 – 1998 was, in my opinion, a really great time to visit this wonderful country. I am forever indebted to my fellow travellers who helped to take some of these photographs in this book, and to the experiences gained during my, 'Camp America' Camp Counsellor role that I undertook before my travels commenced. Thank-you!

So here we are nearly 25 years later, in the year 2021, with the USA and the Wider World being a somewhat different kind of place. Even so, whatever kind of world unfolds over these next few years it is my sincere hope that:

"The USA can also be discovered by all fellow travellers and adventurers, of all ages and backgrounds, and that you too can gain many wonderful, happy memories that will last a lifetime!"

With Best Wishes.

Carl R. Hussey, 2021.

4.

Contents.

1. My USA Photographs, mainly from my 1997 (first) trip.

2. A few of my favourite USA Photographs, mainly from my 1998 (second) trip.

3. A few, 'Final Thoughts'.

4. Useful Books, Websites & Other Resources.

5. For your Notes.

1. My USA Photographs, mainly from my 1997 (first) trip.

1.1 Boston.

We begin with Boston, capital of the state of Massachusetts, which is a city steeped in history. The English settlers who first came here in the mid 17th century named their new home after the birthplace of one of their leaders, Boston in Lincolnshire, England. Governor John Winthrop made Boston capital of the new colony and by the middle of the 18th century Boston was the largest and most important town in North America. However, Boston soon became the main centre of opposition to the mother country and became the starting point of the American War of Independence. It was also the scene of the Boston Massacre and the Boston Tea Party. During the War of Independence, Boston was occupied by British troops, until 4th March 1776 when George Washington's forces drove the British out. Soon after the United States achieved independence. Our first photo is of the John Hancock Building and the Boston Holocaust Memorial:

The 241 metre high John Hancock Building and the Holocaust Memorial.

Christopher Columbus Park.

Harvard University: The oldest university in the United States (founded 1636) at which Presidents John Adams, Theodore Roosevelt, Franklin D. Roosevelt and John F. Kennedy were students.

At the State House, built in 1795 and Park Street Church, built in 1809.

**The Old State House, Boston's oldest public building (1713). This was the
seat of the British colonial government and from the balcony John Adams
read out the Declaration of Independence in 1776
&
Faneuil Hall, built in 1742 as a market and meeting hall.**

<u>Paul Revere House: Built in 1680 this is the oldest wooden structure still standing in Boston. Paul Revere, famed for his ride to Lexington to warn the patriots of an impending British attack, lived here from 1770-1800</u>
<u>&</u>
<u>Old North Church or Christ Church: Boston's oldest church (1723) where in 1775 two lanterns displayed in the steeple signalled that British troops were proceeding to Lexington "by sea".</u>

On the way back from Boston I also visited Newport, Rhode Island which is an exclusive summer resort and where John F. Kennedy and Jacqueline Kennedy spent their honeymoon.

1.2 New York City.

A great deal of my time during 1997 and 1998 was spent working as a Camp Counsellor at a Summer Camp in Brewster, New York, north of New York City. Due to copyright restrictions and photographic permissions etc I unfortunately cannot show these pictures from my work. This is also the case for some of my fellow traveller group photographs taken during my travels. However, my own individual pictures I feel are more than adequate to tell my story and we continue with New York City, the largest city in the USA and a cultural Mecca without equal! The city is a very interesting mosaic of nations and a city of stark social contrasts, in which extravagant luxury and the bitterest of poverty are often only a street apart. From the photographs you will see that New York is probably the most interesting and exciting city on earth!

The Statue of Liberty: There she stands holding her torch aloft and for millions of immigrants the first they saw of America and the symbol of their hopes. The 93 metre high figure was a gift from France to commemorate the 100th anniversary of the United States.

The front and back of the Statue of Liberty.

Ellis Island: Before entering the United States all new immigrants were required to pass through admission procedures on Ellis Island. By the beginning of the First World War some 17 million people had been processed here. Their fate was often decided in a few minutes, so that Ellis Island became known as the "island of tears."

The western half of the southern tip of Manhattan is occupied by Battery Park, with the Castle Clinton National Monument, completed in 1811.

The 1380ft/420m high twin towers of the World Trade Center were opened in 1973 and are New York's highest buildings. As a visitor I was taken up to the observation deck on the 110th floor where the views were spectacular!

The Twin Towers of The World Trade Center in 1997 & The Sphere sculpture at the complex.

The Events of 9/11, (September 11th 2001) and the destruction of this complex and the Twin Towers of the World Trade Center is something that I will never, ever forget. I had just gotten back from a job interview in my home-town of Stoke-on-Trent, UK and proceeded to watch in horror events unfold on my television screen, on that fateful day. I am now one of the rare, very few people in the world that has actually been to the Observation Deck on the top of the South Tower of the Twin Towers, and so their destruction, and the tragic loss of life, holds a special meaning and significance to me.

May all of the victims truly RIP and may something like this never, ever happen again. The following few photographs were the spectacular views to be seen of New York City from the top of the South Tower. These pictures now play their part in the historical documentation of these buildings and their sad passing.

<u>Views of the Statue of Liberty, Ellis Island and Governor's Island.</u>

Other views including Brooklyn and the Brooklyn Bridge.

**<u>The lower Manhattan skyline as seen from the Staten Island Ferry and the
Manhattan Bridge.</u>**

21. <u>The lower Manhattan skyline, a magnificent ship sailing in the East River with the South Ferry Plaza in the background and the Port Authority Downtown Heliport.</u>

<u>The Brooklyn Bridge is the oldest bridge over the East River (1867-83) and was the first to be suspended on steel cables.</u>

<u>Please note that the dates: 1867-83 denote the Brooklyn Bridge construction dates.</u>

23.   **<u>The Empire State Building: Overlooking Midtown Manhattan.</u>**

**<u>The United Nations Headquarters including the Secretariat Building,
the General Assembly Building and an interesting mosaic.</u>**

The Rockefeller Centre (named after John D. Rockefeller Jr) is the world's largest commercial and entertainment complex. Its lively centrepiece is the Rockefeller Plaza with its Sunken Plaza and gilded figure of Prometheus.

1.3 Washington, D.C.

Washington D.C. is the capital of the United States (USA) and is the seat of the Congress and the President of the United States. The city was founded and built for one purpose alone; to provide an independent place for the work of government. It strikes many visitors as being an untypical American city, for there are no skyscrapers, which indeed are prohibited by law. The townscape of Washington, as you will see, is one of classical-style buildings, some of them giant in size, laid out along avenues of enormous width. This has earned Washington the name of the, 'city of magnificent distances.' At the time of my visit, Bill Clinton, was the 42nd President of the United States.

Situated on the 100ft/30m high Capitol Hill, is the United States Capitol, seat of the House of Representatives and the Senate (View of the front).

The back of the United States Capitol, and a typical avenue in Washington DC with the Capitol in the distance.

Standing on the marble terrace, at the rear front of the United States Capitol overlooking the Mall.

The Library of Congress, the largest library in the world, with some
90 million volumes.

Please note that some of the text has been taken from my 1997-1998 photographic albums.

The Supreme Court of the United States, with its large courtroom in which the nine judges of the Supreme Court hold their sessions.

<u>The huge Union Station.</u>

The Mall, along which are most of the museums of the Smithsonian
Institution &
The National Holocaust Memorial Museum, which adjoins the Bureau of
Engraving and Printing, the federal printing office in which bank notes,
stamps and state documents are printed.

A total of 14 museums in Washington are run by the Smithsonian, whose headquarters are in the Castle, a striking building of 1856 in the style of a Norman castle, &
The National Museum of American History.

Some of the typical modern-style buildings to be found in Washington DC.

Please note that there are now 19 museums in the Smithsonian, as of 2021.

The Washington Monument, as seen from the Mall and the Lincoln Memorial. Notice how the obelisk is beautifully mirrored in the Reflecting Pool.

The city's dominant landmark, the 555ft/169m high Washington Monument, an obelisk of Maryland marble is a fitting memorial to George Washington, "father of the nation." A lift takes visitors up to the observation platform, from which there are superb views of the capital and the surrounding area.

The Lincoln Memorial.

The interior of the Lincoln Memorial is dominated by a 20ft/6m high seated figure of Lincoln, looking rather sternly past the Washington Monument towards the Capitol. On the walls are extracts from Lincoln's most celebrated speeches &
The Jefferson Memorial, erected in 1943 on the 200th anniversary of the birth of Thomas Jefferson, one of the authors of the Declaration of Independence.

The Vietnam Veterans Memorial, commemorating the Americans who died in the Vietnam War. On a long wall faced with marble slabs are inscribed the names of the 58,156 US citizens who were killed or reported missing in Vietnam between 1959 and 1975 &
The Korean War Veterans Memorial, honouring members of the US Armed Forces who served in the Korean War, 1950-53.

On Pennsylvania Avenue is the White House, the official residence of the President of the United States. As with the Capitol, the best known aspect of the White House, familiar from many television reports, is the rear front. (A close up view and a distance view).

Arlington National Cemetery serves as a burial place for citizens of the United States, particularly soldiers, who had deserved well of their country. Most visitors find their way past the endless rows of white headstones to the grave of President John F. Kennedy, at which burns the eternal flame. Above the cemetery is Arlington House from which there is a fantastic view of Washington.

1.4 Colonial Williamsburg.

The Colonial National Historical Park runs for 23 miles along the coast of Virginia, linking three places which played important roles in the history of the United States. Starting from Yorktown, it follows York River, turns inland to Williamsburg and ends in Jamestown, on the James River. Colonial Williamsburg, a town founded in 1633 was capital of the colony and for a time capital of the state of Virginia. Its great charm lies not only in the 88 restored and over 50 reconstructed 18th century buildings, but also because it is a living museum, whose, 'inhabitants' wearing period costume, go about their daily business re-creating the pattern of life in colonial Virginia.

Some of the 18th century buildings in Colonial Williamsburg.

The Capitol (1705), scene of the open-air theatrical performance "Prelude to Independence" where visitors celebrate, with the Fife and Drum Corps the *first* declaration of independence.

43.

1.5 Florida.

On the east coast of Florida is Cape Canaveral, home to NASA's Kennedy Space Center. From this rocket-testing site, established in 1949, the first men were launched into orbit and sent to the moon, and from here, the US space shuttle used to be launched. The world famous Walt Disney World in Orlando, Florida, also opened in 1971, and is probably the largest entertainment complex in the world. It is made up of four theme parks: The Magic Kingdom, The EPCOT Center, The Disney Hollywood Studios and The Disney Animal Kingdom. EPCOT: The Experimental Prototype Community of Tomorrow is devoted to the past achievements and the future of technology, with the World Showcase offering a kind of permanent World's Fair.

At the Kennedy Space Center & meeting a "spaceman".

In the Rocket Garden are displayed various types of spacecraft, including the rockets that launched some of the early space shots.

At Shuttle Plaza there is full scale, walk through Space Shuttle and orbiter model, together with the large external fuel tank (ET) with its two solid rocket boosters (SRBs).

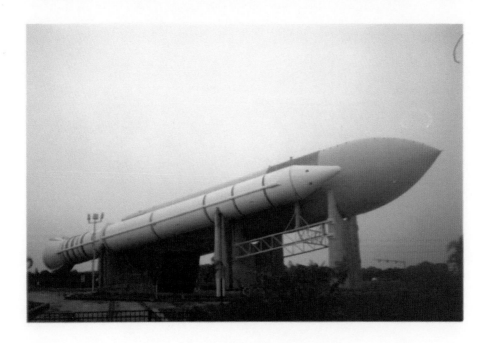

At the Innoventions pavilion in EPCOT's Future World you can play hundreds of the latest video games, including Sonic the Hedgehog!

The Universe of Energy & The Wonders of Life pavilions.

The Land pavilion investigates the production of food, with the Listen to the Land boat ride exploring the history and possible future of farming.

Finally, the Living Seas pavilion takes visitors on a simulated journey deep under the sea.

<u>Japan, overlooking the World Showcase lagoon with Spaceship Earth in the distance &</u>
<u>The American Adventure.</u>

1.6 New Orleans.

After passing through the states of Florida, Alabama and Mississippi, deep in the land of Dixie, we arrive at New Orleans, the largest city in the state of Louisiana. The city's French Quarter is the home of jazz, which was created around the turn of the late 19th century and the early 20th century. Other music such as Blues and Dixieland, ragtime and swing, Creole jazz, and the more recent funky jazz can be heard in Preservation Hall and countless other nightspots. The high spot in the city's programme of festivals is the Carnival (Mardi Gras), during which the French Quarter is taken over by the revellers, with a series of lively parades and masked balls.

Passing through the state of Mississippi on the way to New Orleans & Jackson Square in the French Quarter of New Orleans, with an equestrian statue (1856) of General Andrew Jackson, who in 1815 inflicted a decisive defeat on British forces near the town.

In the French Quarter of New Orleans the French influence is particularly marked in the buildings, some of them between 100 and 260 years old.

A small group of musical performers on Royal Street &
The centre of entertainment in the city, Bourbon Street.

1.7 San Antonio, Texas.

San Antonio, originally a Spanish foundation, reflects more clearly than any other Texan city the influence of different cultures on the history of the state of Texas. On the east side of the city, on Alamo Plaza, is the most famous building in the whole of Texas, the Alamo. The Alamo church was built in 1744 and made into a fort in 1836. In that year, during the Texan war of independence, a small Texan force entrenched themselves in the Alamo against a Mexican army of 3,000 men; and all 187 defenders were killed. Thereafter the Alamo became the, 'cradle of Texan independence,' and, "Remember the Alamo!" became the Texan battle-cry. In April 1836 Texas achieved its independence from Mexico, and until the incorporation of Texas into the United States in 1845, San Antonio belonged to the independent republic of Texas.

The Shrine of the Alamo and the Sales Museum at San Antonio.

1.8 Carlsbad Caverns, Roswell & Santa Fe, New Mexico.

The Carlsbad Caverns lie in south-western New Mexico, on the northern edge of the arid Chihuahua region; a desert area covered with thorny scrub. The Carlsbad Caverns are one of the largest and most impressive cave systems in the world, notable for the variety and beauty of their stalactites and stalagmites and as the home of great swarms of bats.

Roswell is famed for the UFO crash of 1947; and Santa Fe, the capital of the state of New Mexico gains its particular atmosphere from the mingling of Native American Indian, Spanish / Mexican and Anglo-American cultural influences. Around Santa Fe are a number of settlements of Pueblo Indians, where old traditions are still maintained, including ritual dances and artistic craft work.

New Mexico scenery.

56.

White's City, New Mexico and me sitting an a sharp cactus, with Walnut Canyon, a part of the Carlsbad Caverns National Park in the distance.

Pretending to sit on a sharp cactus!

Taking the 1 mile Natural Entrance route into the Carlsbad Caverns. This tour follows the traditional explorer's route, entering the cavern through the large historic natural entrance.

The "Fairyland" rock formations, which are popcorn covered stalagmites
&
The evening flight of the bats of Carlsbad Cavern is a natural phenomenon as fascinating as the cave itself. In a mass exodus at dusk, thousands of Mexican free-tail bats fly from the cave's Natural Entrance for a night of feasting on insects.

On the way to Santa Fe we went to the city of Roswell, famed for the supposedly crashed UFO that was found here in 1947. Roswell has many shops that are devoted to the UFO phenomenon.

The fascinating International UFO Museum & Research Center allows you to look at particular materials and information that are relevant to "The 1947 Roswell Incident."

Another little alien! &
There's lots of UFO and alien memorabilia to be purchased at the gift
shop.

The equipment used by the local Roswell radio station that first broke the news that a crashed UFO had been found near Roswell & Fragments allegedly recovered from the UFO crash site.

Please note that these museum artefacts are mainly just replicas.

<u>**The picturesque streets, low adobe buildings and beautiful churches to be found in Santa Fe.**</u>

**The Santa Fe Village Shopping Plaza &
A group of Indians playing traditional style music.**

The State Capitol, a striking circular building (1966) modelled on an Indian kiva (cult building) &
The main entrance of the State Capitol with the Great Seal of the State of New Mexico and its Indian statue.

1.9 The Mesa Verde, Colorado.

We pass through some beautiful Rocky Mountain scenery in Colorado on the way to the Mesa Verde ('Green Table.') The Mesa Verde is a tabular hill covered with coniferous forest, which reaches a height of 8573ft / 2613m above the semi-desertic foreland of the Rockies in south-western Colorado. It is of interest, not so much for the natural landscape, as for the relics of a past Indian culture, the Anasazi Indians from the 11th century. Here considerable remains of rock habitations, (pit houses on the plateau; cliff dwellings on the sides of the canyons), have been preserved.

Some of the rocks, with their light and dark reddish tones, to found in Southwest Colorado.

There are also some quite bizarre rock formations to be found in the area.

The Mesa Verde.

There are an estimated 4000 statutorily protected archaeological sites in the Mesa Verde National Park, such as the Spruce Tree House, the best preserved cliff dwelling in the park and one of the largest, with 114 rooms and 8 kivas.

Standing at the edge of Soda Canyon, near the Cliff Palace, which with 299 rooms is the largest cave settlement in the park, and was the first to be discovered in 1888.

The Cliff Palace.

1.10 Monument Valley, Arizona.

North-east Arizona is home to the Navajo Indians, a native American tribe with a rich culture, beautiful artwork and a proud history. In their reservation lies Monument Valley Tribal Park, a landscape of brilliant red-rock mesas and towers made famous in countless old western films. I went horse riding through the park and spent the night, under the stars, with the Navajo Indians. This was a very special experience indeed, and I will never forget the experiences and memories that I made here.

A distance view of Monument Valley.

<u>The Monument Valley Tribal Park Visitors Center &</u> <u>The Mitten Campground.</u>

**On my horse, ready to go riding through Monument Valley &
A view of the formations of Redrock called The Mittens.**

A close up view of The Mittens.

<u>A low cloud covering part of the rock formation &</u>
<u>On my horse looking at The Totems.</u>

**From North Window, the huge, dynamic and overpowering scope of
Monument Valley spreads into what seems interminable distance beyond.**

1.11 The Grand Canyon, Arizona.

The Grand Canyon, in north-west Arizona was created by the Colorado River and was described by the Scottish-born pioneer of conservation, and the, 'Father of the National Park System,' John Muir, as the grandest place on God's earth. The breathtaking width and depth of this canyon, its beauty, its forms and colours, leave even the most travelled visitor lost in admiration. During my visit I hiked down the Bright Angel Trail to the bottom of the canyon and took a helicopter ride over the North Rim of the canyon, which was a truly memorable experience!

<u>At the Grand Canyon we took the East Rim Drive, which is where I got my first views of the Canyon.</u>

<u>Hiking down the Bright Angel Trail.</u>

<u>The trail leads to Plateau Point from where you can see the Colorado River running through the Grand Canyon.</u>

Mule riders on the South Kaibab Trail &
Finally after hiking more than 17 miles I reach the top of the Grand Canyon,
where I am totally exhausted!

<u>Before travelling to Las Vegas I took a Papillon Grand Canyon Helicopter tour over the North Rim.</u>

Flying over the spectacular scenery of the Grand Canyon.

1.12 Las Vegas, Nevada.

Las Vegas, the, 'world's largest gambling den,' and the largest city in the state of Nevada, lies in a pale brown desert landscape surrounded by barren hills. The power provided by the massive Hoover Dam enabled Las Vegas to become a city of light, flashing with gaudy neon signs. The 2.5 mile long central section of Las Vegas Boulevard which runs through the city, known as The Strip, is lined with huge entertainment palaces with with revue theatres, night spots, bars, casinos and luxury hotels set in beautiful gardens.

Before arriving in Las Vegas we visited the Hoover Dam, built between 1931 and 1935. This gigantic structure (380m wide and 221m high), which dams the Colorado River to form Lake Mead, serves as a hydroelectric power station.

86.

On the Las Vegas Strip is the Luxor Hotel & Casino, a 30-storey pyramid opened in 1993, with 2526 rooms and a covered water park called "Grand Slam Canyon."

A day and night view of the Excalibur hotel, which is based on the legend of King Arthur.

A day and night view of the hotel New York-New York, which is where the biggest slot jackpot ever at $12,510,559.22 was won, on the 14th April 1997! The hotel also has its own roller coaster running around the outside, the Manhattan Express!

As of 2021, the largest winning Las Vegas slot jackpot now stands at just under $40,000,000!

<u>A day and night view of The Mirage hotel.</u>

1.13 Los Angeles & San Francisco, California.

After leaving Las Vegas and crossing the Mojave Desert we arrive in, 'The City of Angels,' Los Angeles, situated on the Pacific Ocean and Coast in southern California. Los Angeles is the centre of the largest conurbation in the United States, after New York City, with a population of approximately 19 million and covering a total area of about 460 square miles. The city is bounded on the north-east by mountains, and on many days in the year lies under a cloud of smog. Los Angeles is made up of many districts, the most famous of which are Hollywood, the world centre of the film and television industry, and Beverly Hills, where the stars of film and show-business have their luxury. The main attraction in North Hollywood is Universal Studios, an extensive film city with studios and of course, there is also Disneyland in Anaheim, established in 1955.

In the Hollywood Hills there is a magnificent view of Los Angeles, although in the distance the downtown area is covered by a blanket of smog.

In Hollywood, along Hollywood Boulevard is Mann's Chinese Theater. This movie house in the style of a Chinese pagoda, is probably the most famous cinema in the world. In the forecourt are the footprints and handprints of over 150 stars.

The Civic Center of Beverly Hills, home to the Beverly Hills Police Department and Beverly Hills Fire Department.

The Beverly Hills Police Department.

The Beverly Hills Fire Department.

Typical streets in Beverly Hills.

**Located near to Universal Studios, Hollywood are the Hannah-Barbera
cartoon studios &
The main entrance to Universal Studios.**

Views of the Lower Lot, with its huge sound stages at Universal Studios.

Views of Hollywood from the Upper Lot of Universal Studios.

<u>Having my photograph taken at Universal Studios, from the classic 1991 film: Terminator 2: Judgement Day!</u>

The main attraction in Anaheim is Disneyland, a huge theme park established in 1955, which was intended to be, according to its founder Walt Disney, the "happiest place on earth." For the more than 10 million people who come here annually this is exactly what Disneyland represents and today Disneyland ranks as the single top attraction in the state of California. Pictured is the main entrance to the park, with one of the trains of the Disneyland Railroad.

A statue of Walt Disney and Mickey Mouse with a plaque that reads:
"PARTNERS, I think most of all what I want Disneyland to be is a happy place...
where parents and children can have fun together." &
Sleeping Beauty's Castle in Fantasyland.

<u>Meeting Mickey Mouse in Mickey's House in Mickey's Toontown!</u>

We now arrive at our final destination of my 1997 USA travels; San Francisco, 'everyone's favourite city,' situated at the, 'Golden Gate' to the Pacific Ocean in northern California. It is built on more than 40 hills on a 7.5 mile wide peninsula between the open sea and San Francisco Bay. The expanses of water surrounding the city have a moderating effect on the climate, which has a mildness of spring all year round.

The Golden Gate Bridge; one of the largest and handsomest suspension bridges in the world, spans the Golden Gate, the narrow strait between the San Francisco peninsula and the Marin peninsula, linking San Francisco with Marin County.

The first exit on the Marin side of the bridge, Vista Point, provides outstanding views of the San Francisco skyline.

The bridge is often shrouded in thick fog.

<u>At San Francisco International Airport, preparing to fly home to London on</u>
<u>the Virgin Atlantic 747 jumbo jet &</u>
<u>My final view of the USA as the sun sets in the distance.</u>

2. A few of my favourite USA Photographs, mainly from my 1998 (second) trip.

2.1 Independence Hall, Philadelphia.

2.2 Niagara Falls, USA / Canada.

2.3 Chicago, Illinois.

2.4 Badlands National Park, South Dakota.

2.5 The Crazy Horse Memorial, South Dakota.

2.6 The Mount Rushmore National Memorial, South Dakota.

2.7 Devils Tower National Monument, Wyoming.

2.8 Yellowstone National Park, Wyoming.

2.9 The Bonneville Salt Flats, Utah.

120.

2.10 Yosemite National Park, California.

3. A few, 'Final Thoughts.'

I want to thank-you for reading my book, 'A Photographic Journey around the USA (1997 – 1998)'. I hope that I have provided you with a little inspiration to explore this wonderful country for yourself, and to help to protect it for future generations; especially America's very precious National Parks. There are so many happy and significant memories that I have shared with people about my travels over the last 25 years, and I hope that this book will now serve as a reminder of these travel memories. I would like to close with a few choice quotations / rules of conduct from President Abraham Lincoln, the highly esteemed 16th President of the United States. The quotes are mainly from the Lincoln Memorial, in Washington D.C. I hope that you find them to be of some use in these somewhat, 'interesting and changing' times.

Abraham Lincoln's Rules of Conduct.

Better to remain silent and be thought a fool than to speak out and remove all doubt.

The fact is, truth is your truest friend, no matter what the circumstances are.

Leave nothing for tomorrow which can be done today.

I say, "try." If we never try, we shall never succeed.

Stand with anybody that stands right. Stand with him while he is right, and part with him when he goes wrong.

Thank-you once again and may I wish you a very happy and safe future travelling experience!

4. Useful Books, Websites and Other Resources.

Please see the Amazon website for a very wide variety of USA Travel Books. The DK Eyewitness Travel books on the USA, I have also found to be very useful.

USA travel and tourist information can also be found via a GOOGLE internet search etc, and I have always found the www.visitusa.org.uk , www.visittheusa.co.uk , and the www.nps.gov websites to be very helpful.

Other resources and information can be found at your local library, and also via the TV and other media sources etc. Thank-you.

Happy Travels!

With Best Wishes.

Carl R. Hussey, B.A. PGCert.

5. For your Notes.

Printed in Great Britain
by Amazon

22825120R00073